Judaism

Major World Religions

Buddhism	Islam
Christianity	Judaism
Hinduism	Sikhism

MAJOR WORLD RELIGIONS

Judaism

Adam Lewinsky

MASON CREST
PHILADELPHIA

Mason Crest
450 Parkway Drive, Suite D
Broomall, PA 19008
www.masoncrest.com

©2018 by Mason Crest, an imprint of National Highlights, Inc.

Printed and bound in the United States of America.

CPSIA Compliance Information: Batch #MWR2017.
For further information, contact Mason Crest at 1-866-MCP-Book.

First printing
1 3 5 7 9 8 6 4 2

Library of Congress Cataloging-in-Publication Data

on file at the Library of Congress
ISBN: 978-1-4222-3820-2 (hc)
ISBN: 978-1-4222-7973-1 (ebook)

Major World Religions series ISBN: 978-1-4222-3815-8

Table of Contents

KEY ICONS TO LOOK FOR:

Words to understand: These words with their easy-to-understand definitions will increase the reader's understanding of the text while building vocabulary skills.

Sidebars: This boxed material within the main text allows readers to build knowledge, gain insights, explore possibilities, and broaden their perspectives by weaving together additional information to provide realistic and holistic perspectives.

Educational Videos: Readers can view videos by scanning our QR codes, providing them with additional educational content to supplement the text. Examples include news coverage, moments in history, speeches, iconic sports moments and much more!

Text-dependent questions: These questions send the reader back to the text for more careful attention to the evidence presented there.

Research projects: Readers are pointed toward areas of further inquiry connected to each chapter. Suggestions are provided for projects that encourage deeper research and analysis.

Series glossary of key terms: This back-of-the book glossary contains terminology used throughout this series. Words found here increase the reader's ability to read and comprehend higher-level books and articles in this field.

Jews gather to pray at the Western Wall, the remains of an ancient limestone wall that was part of the Jewish Temple in Jerusalem. It is considered one of the holiest places in Judaism.

 # Words to Understand in This Chapter

commandments—613 commandments can be found in the Torah; the passage known as the Ten Commandments summarizes them. See mitzvah.

Gemara—another term for the Mishnah and the Talmud.

halakhah—Jewish religious law.

Messiah—a person that, according to Jewish belief, God will send into the world to free the Jews from oppression.

Mishnah—the written form of oral explanations of the Torah and other teachings, which, together with the Gemara, forms the Talmud.

mitzvah—a commandment (plural *mitzvot*).

oral Torah—explanations of the meaning of the written Torah given to Moses when he received the written Torah.

Talmud—writings composed of the Mishnah and the Gemara that are studied and used to determine the meaning of the Torah.

Tanakh—The Hebrew scriptures, a collection of twenty-four ancient texts that Jews consider to be sacred. Often referred to in English as the Hebrew Bible.

Torah—the first five books of the Hebrew Bible. These are believed to have been revealed to Moses on Mount Sinai. Also known as the "written Torah."

A Jewish man reads a holy book in a synagogue in the historic Neve Tzedek district of Tel Aviv. Israel is the only country in the world with a predominantly Jewish population.

1 What Do Jews Believe?

Judaism is more than a religion. It is also a way of living and thinking, a body of literature, a society, a musical tradition, a language, and a history that stretches back over 4,000 years. It is built upon a code of beliefs, laws, and teachings that are set out in the *Tanakh* (also called the Hebrew Bible) and other Jewish religious texts. The laws and customs of Judaism have provided the framework for a practical and spiritual way of life for its followers since the origins of Judaism thousands of years ago.

There are three basic principles of faith at the heart of Judaism—God, the *Torah*, and the land of Israel. First, Jews believe there is only one God, the creator, who is eternal, all-powerful, all-knowing, and loving. Judaism was the original monotheistic religion—the first to teach that there is only one God.

Second, Jews believe the word of God was revealed directly to the prophet Moses on Mount Sinai and was written down by him as the five books of the Torah. The Torah contains many of the laws that Jews live by, such as the Ten Commandments.

Third, Jews believe that God made a covenant, or agreement, with their ancestors, choosing them to be a "kingdom of priests and a holy people." As part of this agreement, they believe God promised to give them an area of land that lies along the eastern shore of the Mediterranean Sea. This "Promised Land" of Israel includes the city of Jerusalem and was the site of the ancient Jewish kingdom. It roughly corresponds to the modern-day state of Israel, which was established after the end of the Second World War, in 1948.

Being God's "chosen people" does not mean that Jews consider themselves superior to others, however. Jews believe that everyone is created in God's image. It follows from this that all people are created equal, and therefore no person or nation can be superior to any other.

Jewish people believe that one day, God will send a special leader: the *Messiah*, who will unite people and lead the world into a new age of peace, justice, and equal rights for all. The word "Messiah" comes from the Hebrew word *mashiah*, which means "anointed one." In ancient times, Jewish kings and high priests were anointed with oil when they came into power, showing that they had been chosen by God for a special purpose. Jews believe that the Messiah

A menorah, a seven–branched candelabrum, is the traditional symbol of Judaism, recalling the one in the ancient Temple in Jerusalem.

Judaism puts great importance on education. Here, a girl in cheder *(a Sunday morning religious class) practices writing a phrase in the Hebrew alphabet.*

will be a human leader who is descended from King David, an important figure in Jewish history. Jews believe the Messiah's arrival will bring about the restoration of the Temple in Jerusalem and all its rituals, and will also mark the establishment of God's Kingdom on Earth.

Jewish Holy Writings

The most important Jewish holy text is the Tanakh, or Hebrew Bible. It is a collection of 39 books divided into three parts—the Torah, the Prophets, and the Writings.

The Torah is composed of the Five Books of Moses—known as Genesis, Exodus, Leviticus, Numbers, and

Deuteronomy. The Greek word *Pentateuch* ("five scrolls") is also used to refer to these five books, which were originally written on scrolls. Jews believe that the Torah was revealed by God directly to Moses.

Although the Torah is changeless, because it is the word of God, progressive Judaism teaches that people's circumstances, ideas, and values change as generations come and go. Therefore the interpretation of the Torah changes with the passage of time.

Copies of the Torah that are read in synagogues are handwritten and stored on scrolls. The reader uses a pointer, called yad, *so that he or she does not touch the scroll.*

Educational Video

Scan here to hear the first chapter of the Torah being read in the Hebrew language.

Jews sometimes use the word *Torah* to refer to the entire Bible, or even the entirety of Jewish teaching in all its forms.

The second section of the Tanakh is called *Nevi'im*, or "the Prophets." Prophets were people who received God's word directly and so spoke with divine inspiration. They expressed God's will for the people. The Prophets section includes some texts that provide the history about the ancient Israelites, their conquest of the land of Israel (then called Canaan) after the death of Moses around 1500 BCE, and the rise and fall of the kingdom of Israel established by King David around 1000 BCE. It also includes the writings of prophets who criticized the Jewish people for failing to live up to their part of the covenant with God, and predicted things that would happen to the Jewish people in the future—including the coming of the Messiah.

The final section of the Tanakh is the *Ketuvim*, or "Writings." It contains 13 books of poems, songs, historical stories, and wise sayings.

Understanding the Scriptures

Jews believe that when Moses was given the Torah on Mount Sinai, God spent 40 days explaining how to understand and interpret the scriptures and the laws they contained. These instructions, called the *oral Torah*, were passed on by word of mouth from Moses to Joshua, his successor as leader of the Israelites. They continued to be passed down by the Jewish priests, prophets, and elders over many generations.

These oral teachings and traditions were brought together in a single written work called the *Mishnah* (meaning "learning by repetition,") which was further interpreted in a second work called the *Gemara* ("study"). The Mishnah and Gemara together are called the *Talmud* ("instruction"). The Talmud is nearly 2,000 years old, but

A typical page of the Talmud covers many centuries of Jewish religious scholarship. The original Torah law or statement is placed in a box centered on the page, with commentary from revered rabbis surrounding it.

it is still studied today with the Bible, and still serves as a guide to Jewish law and traditional Jewish life.

Jewish Law

The body of Jewish Law is called *halakhah*. A literal translation of this Hebrew word would be something like "to travel" or "to follow a path." Jews believe that the law shows them the correct path to follow through life. *Halakhah* began with the Torah, the part of the Bible given to Moses and interpreted in the Talmud, but it has evolved and grown since then. It now comprises three elements.

The first is the *mitzvot*. These are the 613 *commandments* written in the Torah. The Rabbis divided them into 248 positive and 365 negative *mitzvot*. A positive *mitzvah* (the singular of *mitzvot*) is a divine instruction to do some-

This archaeological model shows what the Second Temple in Jerusalem probably looked like. The Second Temple was built in the sixth century BCE, expanded during the rule of Herod the Great in the first century BCE, and destroyed by Roman armies in 70 CE. Without the temple, Jews cannot comply with many of the Torah laws that require animal sacrifice.

The Ten Commandments

According to the Torah, the Ten Commandments were inscribed by God on two stone tablets. The Ten Commandments are the basis of Jewish Law, and are listed twice in the Torah, in the books of Exodus and Deuteronomy. Although Jews and Christians both consider these books to be sacred, they differ on exactly how the commandments are numbered. The Jewish numbering of the ten commandments is as follows:

1. I am the Lord your God, who brought you out of the land of Egypt, out of the house of bondage.
2. You shall have no other gods before me. You shall not make for yourself graven images, or bow down to idols or serve them.
3. You shall not take the name of the Lord your God in vain.
4. Remember Shabbat day, to keep it holy. Six days you shall labor and do all your work, but the seventh day is a Shabbat to the Lord your God; on it you shall not do any work.
5. Honor your father and mother.
6. You shall not kill.
7. You shall not commit adultery.
8. You shall not steal.
9. You shall not bear false witness against your neighbor.
10. You shall not covet your neighbor's goods or wife.

thing—you shall give to charity according to your means, for example. A negative *mitzvah* is a prohibition, such as, you shall not bear a grudge or, you shall not steal. Some positive and negative *mitzvot* duplicate each other. The Tanakh instructs Jews to rest on Shabbat, as well as not to work on Shabbat—these separate *mitzvah* effectively mean the same thing. All of the 613 mitzvot are considered to be equally important and equally sacred, no matter how trivial or mundane they may seem to be.

The second element of the Law is composed of guidelines and restrictions added later by the teachers who composed the Talmud. For example, the Tanakh provides the mitzvah that Jews must not work on Shabbat, but in the Talmud many different types of work are analyzed so that Jews can understand exactly what they are or are not permitted to do on Shabbat. So for example, on Shabbat a Jewish person could eat raw vegetables, such as in a salad. However, they could not cook the vegetables before eating them, as the Talmud considers the act of cooking to be work.

Jews believe that all of the Torah's laws still apply. However, some of them are impossible to observe today because they relate to activities, situations, or places that no longer exist. These include laws governing animal sacrifices (which must be performed in the Jerusalem Temple, which was destroyed in 70 CE) or laws that relate to a theocratic state of Israel that is governed by priests (the modern State of Israel is, technically, a secular democracy, although most residents are Jewish). Some of the laws of the Torah only apply within the land of Israel, or to certain people. About 270 of the original 613 *mitzvot* are applicable today to Jews living outside Israel. Only the most Orthodox Jews attempt to observe all of these laws. Other, more liberal Jewish groups observe fewer laws.

There are also many long-standing traditions, customs, and practices that are an important part of the daily lives of some Jews. These are not considered to be as important or as unchangeable as the divine Laws of the Torah.

 ## Text-Dependent Questions

1. What are three basic principles of faith at the heart of Judaism?
2. What is the most important Jewish holy text?
3. What is the body of Jewish Law called?

 ## Research Project

The "documentary hypothesis" is a theory that emerged in the nineteenth century about the authorship of the five books of the Torah: Genesis, Exodus, Leviticus, Deuteronomy, and Numbers. According to this theory, these books were not composed by Moses around 1500 BCE, as many Jews had previously believed. Instead, the documentary hypothesis states that each of the five books includes elements of several different ancient writings, which were combined and edited into their current form around 750 BCE in the Kingdom of Israel. Using the internet or your school library, find out more about the documentary hypothesis. Write a two-page paper explaining the hypothesis, and present it to your class.

 Words to Understand in This Chapter

anti-Semitism—discrimination against Jews.

birthright—according to some societies, a right that is given to the oldest child to inherit the largest share of his family's wealth and property.

Conservative—a movement in Judaism that does not require its followers to be as strict as Orthodox Jews.

Reform—a branch of Judaism that believes in updating and reinterpreting Jewish religious laws for life in the modern world, known as the Liberal movement in the United Kingdom.

Zionism—the movement, named after Zion, that campaigned for the establishment of a Jewish homeland in Palestine.

2 The Origins and History of Judaism

The history of Judaism begins with a shepherd called Abram, who lived in southern Mesopotamia (modern-day Iraq) around 4,000 years ago. Abram rejected the worship of idols, which was common at that time. Instead, he believed that everything in existence was made by a single creator. According to the Book of Genesis, the first book of the Torah, God the Creator spoke to Abram and offered to make a covenant, or agreement, with him. If Abram would leave his home in Mesopotamia and go to a new "Promised Land," and if he and his descendants agreed to keep God's laws, then they would create a great nation.

Abram was about 75 years old when he agreed to God's covenant. He spent years traveling through the land of Canaan, as the region between the River Jordan and the eastern Mediterranean Sea was then known. Abram also traveled to Egypt during this time. He was accompanied by his wife, Sarai, and his nephew Lot.

Abram and Sarai had no children, but God had promised that his descendants would be very numerous. Sarai was too old to become pregnant, so Abram's first son was born to his wife's servant, Hagar. This son was named Ishmael. Later, when Ishmael was about twelve years old, God blessed Abram and Sarai with another son. Abram was 100 years old and Sarai was 90 when she became pregnant with a son they called Issac. As a reminder of this blessing, God also changed Abram's name to Abraham, and Sarai's to Sarah at this time. The Torah teaches that Isaac became the successor to Abraham, and inherited his wealth and property.

Like his father, Isaac also had two sons. The oldest was named Esau, and the younger one was named Jacob. Esau was supposed to inherit Isaac's property, but he was not very smart and he agreed to trade his *birthright* to Jacob in exchange for some food. Because of this, Jacob also inherited the promises of God's covenant with Abraham. God eventually changed Jacob's name to Israel, so Jacob's descendants became known as the Children of Israel, or the Israelites. The Israelites were also known in ancient times as the Hebrews.

The Israelites Escape a Famine

Jacob/Israel had twelve sons, named (from first-born to last) Reuben, Simeon, Levi, Judah, Dan, Naphtali, Gad, Asher, Issachar, Zebulun, Joseph, and Benjamin. When

This painting depicts one of the most famous scenes in religious history: an angel stopping Abraham before he can sacrifice his son Isaac on an altar in the mountains. The Torah says that God asked for this sacrifice as a test of Abraham's faith.

Israel treated his second-youngest son Joseph with favoritism, the other brothers became jealous. The Book of Genesis says they beat up Joseph and sold him as a slave to some traders. The traders took Joseph with them to Egypt.

God used this terrible act for good, however. Joseph started out as a slave in the Pharaoh's court, but because he was smart and hard-working, he soon gained an important position in the Egyptian government.

When a terrible famine struck Canaan, Jacob and his family, including his sons, went to Egypt hoping they would not starve. They had no idea Joseph was still alive, and were shocked to find him thriving as the Pharaoh's most trusted advisor. He forgave his brothers, and the Pharaoh invited the Israelites to come and settle in Egypt, where there was food available. Israel, his sons, and their descendants lived comfortably in Egypt for several generations.

While they lived in Egypt, the families of Israel's sons grew and developed into separate tribes of Israelites. Reuben, Simeon, Levi, Judah, Dan, Naphtali, Gad, Asher, Issachar, Zebulun, and Benjamin each founded a tribe. Two of Joseph's sons, Manasseh and Ephraim, each founded tribes, which were sometimes called the "half-tribes." Together, these became known as the Twelve Tribes of Israel.

Israelites in Captivity

The Israelites would remain in Egypt long after the deaths of Joseph and his brothers. The Torah says that the Israelites lived in Egypt for 430 years. Unfortunately, their good situation eventually turned bad when a new pharaoh came to power. He was concerned that the number of Israelites was growing, and didn't want them to become too powerful or prosperous. The pharaoh enslaved the Israelites and put them to work in the fields and on building projects.

To reduce their numbers, the Pharaoh ordered all Israelite boys to be killed at birth. One baby escaped the slaughter by being hidden in a basket at the edge of a river. He was found

According to Jewish legends, called midrash, *the Israelites provided the labor to build some of Egypt's great pyramids and monuments.*

there by the Pharaoh's daughter, given the name Moses, and brought up in the Egyptian royal court. He later discovered he was an Israelite. When he saw an Egyptian treating a Hebrew slave badly, he killed the Egyptian and then fled for his life.

Moses became a shepherd in Midian, a land in the northwestern part of the modern Arabian desert. While he was tending his sheep one day, he was amazed to see a burning bush that was not consumed by the flames, and he heard the voice of God commanding him to return to Egypt and free his people.

Moses did as God told him. He returned to Egypt and demanded that the Pharaoh let the Israelites go free, But the

Plagues in Egypt

According to the Torah, each time Pharaoh refuses to set the Israelites free, God causes a problem in Egypt. Ten plagues are recorded, with each more severe or painful than the last. They included:

1. The River Nile ran red as blood and all the fish died.
2. A plague of frogs.
3. A plague of lice.
4. A plague of flies.
5. A plague of livestock disease.
6. A plague of boils.
7. A plague of hail.
8. A plague of locusts.
9. Darkness descended on the land for three days.
10. The death of the first-born sons of Egypt.

Some commentators have noted that the first nine plagues could all be explained as natural phenomena. For example, "turning the river to blood" may refer to heavy deposits of reddish silt washed down the Nile from Ethiopia or Central Africa; this silt would have been deadly to river-dwelling fish. Hail and swarms of locusts are both events that occur naturally, and are not uncommon in Egypt even today. Darkness over the land might have been caused by an eclipse or a sandstorm. The important thing to remember, Jewish writers note, is that these plagues occurred with unusual rapidity—coming at God's bidding and timing.

Pharaoh refused. God then sent ten plagues to punish the Egyptians. The tenth plague resulted in the death of the first-born son of every Egyptian family. Before this happened, God warned the Israelites, who smeared lamb's blood on their door-posts so that the Angel of Death would pass over them. The Feast of the Passover (known as Pesach in Hebrew) commemorates this event.

The Pharaoh finally let the Israelites go, but then sent an army chasing after them. The Israelites' flight from Egypt under the leadership of Moses is known as the Exodus. God parted the waters of the Red Sea to let the Israelites cross, but brought the water tumbling down on the Egyptian army when it tried to follow them.

This statue—believed to represent the Egyptian pharaoh Ramses II—is located at the Great Temple of Ramses in southern Egypt. A popular tradition holds that Ramses was the pharaoh who kept the Israelites in slavery; however, the true identity of the pharaoh mentioned in the Bible may never be known.

After this, according to the Torah, the Israelites wandered for many years through the desert of the Sinai Peninsula, a region between Egypt and the Promised Land. When the Israelites reached a high point called Mount Sinai, Moses climbed the mountain alone. There he received the Ten Commandments, which were written in stone by God, and other laws for the Israelites.

Regaining the Promised Land

The Torah says that Moses and the Israelites whom he led out of slavery never reached the Promised Land. Instead, they spent 40 years wandering in the Sinai desert. After the death of Moses, the Israelites finally crossed the River Jordan and reached the land of Canaan—the Promised Land. This is believed to have occurred around 1250 BCE.

Canaan was already occupied by a variety of people, known as the Canaanites. They were polytheistic, and worshiped many different gods and goddesses. The Canaanites did not want to share their land—to them, the arrival of the Israelites was an invasion by foreigners, and they resisted fiercely.

The Israelites conquered Canaan under the leadership of Joshua, the successor of Moses. Ten of the 12 tribes settled in the north. The remaining two tribes, Judah and Benjamin, settled in the southern part of Canaan. Each tribe had its own area of territory, which was spelled out in the Torah.

The Jewish scriptures say that God instructed the Israelites to completely destroy the Canaanites and possess the entire land. Today, this order troubles some people, who question how a just and merciful God could support the annihilation of the Canaanites. Theologians speculate that God wanted to keep his chosen people away from the influence of the Canaanites, who worshiped strange but seduc-

Joshua, the successor to Moses, leads the Israelite army in a battle against the Canaanite city of Gibeon. According to the Torah, the Israelites succeeded in conquering most of the Promised Land from the Canaanites.

tive gods that might tempt the Israelites into behavior that would violate their covenant.

In any case, although the Israelites did take control of the land and massacre many people, they did not obey God completely. Some Canaanites were enslaved; others defended their territories or made treaties with the Israelites. The ultimate conquest of Canaan would take several hundred years. Also, as the Israelites observed Canaanite rituals and intermarried into their families, some of the people began to turn away from God, and worshiped the gods revered by their pagan neighbors.

For much of the time the Israelites were fighting for Canaan, wise heroes known as the Judges ruled the people. When the Israelites turned away from God, judges like Deborah, Gideon, and Samson helped bring them back to the true path. Eventually, however, the people of Israel decided that they wanted a king to rule over them, just as the neighboring Canaanite nations did. A man named Saul was anointed the first king of Israel; he ruled from about 1022 to 1000 BCE. After Saul was killed in battle, a young man named David became king.

The Kingdom of Israel

During the reign of King David (1000–961 BCE), Israel achieved its greatest glory and extent. David captured the

An ancient stone altar, probably used for pagan worship, found at Tel Megiddo in modern-day Israel. This Canaanite city was the site of many battles in ancient times.

Tetragrammaton

The tetragrammaton is a term for four Hebrew letters used together in the Tanakh to refer to God: Yod-He-Waw-He. These Hebrew letters are often transliterated into English as YHWH. (In some English-language Bibles they are changed to a form that includes vowels, such as Yahweh.) YHWH is one of the names of God that appears in the Tanakh.

Observant Jews do not pronounce the tetragrammaton, either aloud or to themselves in silence, nor do they read aloud transliterated forms such as Yahweh. Instead, in synagogue readings the word is generally substituted with a different term. Common substitutions for God are *hakadosh baruch hu* ("The Holy One, Blessed Be He"), *Adonai* ("The Lord"), or *HaShem* ("The Name").

city of Jerusalem and made it his capital. David's kingdom covered the area of the modern-day state of Israel, as well as parts of Lebanon, Syria, Jordan, and Iraq. This was a time in ancient history when the traditional regional powers, empires based in Mesopotamia and Egypt, were comparatively weak. As a result Israel, located between these two lands, emerged as the dominant power of its day.

David's son Solomon was considered a wise ruler who maintained the powerful position of Israel. Solomon is also credited with building the enormous Holy Temple in Jerusalem where God was worshiped. But after Solomon's

David was an effective king of Israel, and Jews believe that the Messiah will be his descendant.

death around 922 BCE, the Israelite kingdom became divided. The kingdom of Judah was established in the southern part of the country and included the tribes of Judah and Benjamin. The kingdom of Israel, also known as the Northern Kingdom, included the other ten tribes. Its capital was at the city of Samaria.

Scripture relates that some of the kings who ruled over the two Israelite kingdoms remained faithful to God and His commandments, but that most of the rulers—and most of the people— disobeyed God. In 722 BCE the Northern Kingdom was conquered by the powerful Assyrians, and the ten tribes were dispersed completely. They later became known as the "Ten Lost Tribes." The Jewish people interpreted this calamity as God's punishment for their violations of the covenant.

In the remaining Israelite kingdom of Judah, prophets such as Isaiah and Jeremiah reminded the people and their leaders about the importance of keeping their covenant with God and admonished them to give up their wicked ways. Scripture relates that the Israelites did not listen to the prophets, however. In 586 BCE the Babylonians conquered Judah, taking control over Jerusalem and destroying the Holy Temple. Many of the Israelites were taken as prisoners to Babylon, an ancient city in Mesopotamia.

Judaism Develops in Exile

During the captivity in Babylon, the Israelites' religion underwent significant changes. It was at this point that the religion began to be referred to as Judaism, and the people who practiced it as Jews.

Since the time of Solomon, the Temple in Jerusalem had been a focal point where the entire Israelite community came to worship God and perform the rituals of sacrifice. With the Temple destroyed and the Israelites in exile, new prophets appeared. They explained that no matter where the Jewish people were, they could worship God. They claimed that God had not forgotten His chosen people, and would send a messiah to save them.

The exile forced Jews to reconsider their view of God. In the past, they had worshiped God while at the same time considering the deities of other nations as legitimate. They had sometimes even worshipped other gods along with God. In Babylon, the prophets taught that God controlled all of history, and that there were no other gods or forces that could affect their lives. If the Israelites kept the covenant, the prophets taught, God would save His people from captivity and reestablish a kingdom that would be greater than King David's.

The Jewish communities in Babylon became centered in places of communal prayer, where the priests could teach the laws of the covenant and perform worship ceremonies. These eventually became known as synagogues, and they would become a vital part of Jewish religious life. The synagogues came to be led by teachers known as rabbis.

The Exile Ends

Babylonian rule over the Jews ended in 539 bce when the Persian Empire conquered Babylon. The Persian ruler Cyrus the Great gave the Jews permission to return to Jerusalem. Some did return, but others remained in Babylon. These Jews established themselves in Persian society and business but maintained their religious beliefs.

Tens of thousands of Jews did leave Babylon after 539 and returned to Jerusalem and the surrounding area. Cyrus had ordered them to rebuild the Temple, and the Jews enthusiastically began this project. However, they found themselves fighting people living in northern Canaan, including the Samaritans—descendants of Israelites who had remained in the land after the Babylonian invasion and had intermarried with pagans. This delayed the reconstruction of the Temple, which was not completed for more than 20 years.

In 458 BCE a priest named Ezra led a second group of Jews from Babylon to Jerusalem. On his arrival, Ezra told the Jews of Jerusalem that they needed to follow the law more carefully. He undertook a program of regularly reading the law to the people and explaining how the Jews should behave. Through Ezra's actions the Jews realized that many of God's laws had not been kept for centuries.

For example, the Israelites were supposed to observe a certain festival during the seventh month of the year—the Festival of Tabernacles, or Sukkot. However, the ceremonies had not been performed correctly since shortly after the time of Moses. The Book of Ezra-Nehemiah says that after Ezra taught the people about the law, they observed the festival properly.

Determining exactly how God wanted the Jews to observe His commandments became an important element of Judaism. Priests began to teach the people how the laws should be interpreted and obeyed. From this developed an elaborate legal code of conduct for the Jews to follow. This code was unwritten, because the Jewish priests did not want to imply that their rulings could not change or that they were the equals of God's laws as presented in the Torah. Instead, the priests memorized the laws and the cases that had led to different rulings, passing this information orally to later generations.

Greek and Roman Rule

In 334 BCE, Greek armies led by Alexander the Great invaded Persian-controlled territories. Within ten years, Alexander ruled a vast empire that stretched from Egypt in the west to India in the east. Alexander's conquests had an immediate and lasting impact on the Mediterranean world. The language and practices of the Greeks became dominant throughout his empire. The blending of Greek culture with aspects of the conquered Persian and Asian cultures became known as Hellenism.

For a while, the Jewish people thrived under Greek rule. Alexander and the rulers that followed him allowed the Greeks to keep their cultural and religious traditions. In turn, many Jews admired Greek schools and libraries, philosophical and logical systems, and art.

In 198 BCE a Greek ruling dynasty known as the Seleucids became rulers of Judea, as the Jewish province around Jerusalem was known. They soon began to take away some of the freedoms that Jews had within their empire. They encouraged Jews to accept Greek laws and customs in place of Jewish ones. Around 168 BCE the Seleucid emperor Antiochus IV Epiphanes imposed harsh new restrictions on the residents of Jerusalem. He forbade Jews to observe Shabbat or perform circumcisions, and he erected a statue of himself in the Temple. The emperor's demand to be worshiped as a god was unacceptable, and a Jewish priest named Mattathias and his sons rose up in protest. After four years of fighting, Jewish forces under Judah Maccabee captured Jerusalem, and in December 164 they rededicated the Temple. (The festival of Hannukah commemorates this event.) For about a hundred years, Judea would remain a small, independent kingdom.

In 63 BCE, the Roman Empire claimed Judea as a province. The Romans the installed puppet monarchs (the most famous of these was King Herod, under whose rule the Jewish Temple was renovated and expanded. They also sent Roman governors and soldiers to maintain control.

Roman rule was unpopular. Rome resorted to harsh measures when necessary to maintain control over its vast territories, and it imposed heavy taxes on its subjects. At various times Jews organized into groups to oppose Rome; in response, Roman legions were garrisoned in Jerusalem and elsewhere to prevent rebellion.

Two revolts had dire consequences for the Jews. The first began in 66 CE. It lasted for four years, ending in the year 70 when the Romans sacked Jerusalem. Roman forces destroyed the Temple, massacred thousands of Jews, and enslaved thousands of others. A second major revolt, led by Simon bar Kokhba, erupted in 132 CE. Years of difficult fighting ensued before the Romans finally prevailed in 135. After this, Roman legions destroyed Jerusalem and forced nearly all of the Jews to leave the land. They brought in people from other Roman areas to settle the area, which was renamed Palestine.

Educational Video

For a short video about the Jewish Temple, scan here:

Rabbinic Judaism

Important developments in Judaism ensured the religion's survival after these disasters. At that time most of the Jewish Law had never been written down. Instead, it was carried in the memories of the high priests of the Temple, and handed down from generation to generation. With the Temple destroyed, synagogues became the centers of Jewish religious life. Therefore it was very important that each community's rabbi have a complete understanding of God's law.

During the first century CE, religious leaders agreed on the written scriptures that belonged in the Hebrew Bible; after this no books could be added to the canon. Around 200 CE a rabbi known as Judah the Prince collected and edited the oral law into a text that became known as the Mishnah.

The Mishnah preserved just the oral law, without providing citations from the scriptures to explain the law. Over a period of several hundred years Jewish scholars who had memorized and studied the Torah and Mishnah would create a new text to explain the relationship between the oral law and the Torah. This enormous commentary on the law was called the Talmud.

A Sefer Torah is a handwritten copy of the sacred writings.

Together, the Torah, Mishnah, and Talmud created an authoritative written body of Jewish law and custom. As a result, Jews anywhere in the world could look to the halakhah for guidance. This ensured that Judaism would remain the same no matter where it was practiced, as all rabbis could draw on the same written sources to teach their congregations.

Thus the development of Rabbinic Judaism gave lasting strength to the Jewish faith, saving Judaism from being lost to history like many other ancient religions. Over the centuries the practice of Judaism would undergo changes, and by the nineteenth century the *Reform* and *Conservative* branches of the faith had emerged. Despite changing interpretation, however, the Torah, Mishnah, and Talmud remain the cornerstones of Judaism.

Persecution of Jews

After the Jewish people were forced from their homeland by the Romans, Jewish communities developed in many parts of the empire. However, the Jews often faced persecution. After the fall of the Roman Empire, rivalry between Christianity and Judaism resulted in long-lasting hostility to Jews throughout Europe.

By 1800, most of the world's Jews lived in eastern Europe. They were usually treated as outsiders. There was widespread repression and persecution of Jews in Russia and eastern Europe in the nineteenth century. Massacres known as pogroms led to more than a million Jews leaving for the United States, while others fled to western Europe.

Jewish immigrants to the United States often lived in crowded neighborhoods like this one in New York City.

Small numbers of Jews also began to emigrate from Russia and Europe to Palestine in the late nineteenth century. Palestine at the time was a province under the control of the Ottoman Empire, which was ruled by Muslims. In 1896 a Zionist movement began to campaign for the establishment of a Jewish homeland in Palestine. *Zionism* was named after Zion, the hill on which Jerusalem was built.

After the First World War ended in 1918, Great Britain took control of Palestine. The British supported the creation of a Jewish state there, but Palestinian Arabs resisted the growing numbers of Jewish settlers.

The Holocaust

As fascism spread through Europe during the 1930s, *anti-Semitism* intensified. When the National Socialist (Nazi) party came to power in Germany, they transformed anti-Semitism from religious discrimination to government policy. Jews were officially classified as *Untermenschen* (subhumans) and forced to identify themselves by wearing a yellow badge. Their rights were restricted, their businesses were attacked and their property was confiscated. Shamefully, few governments came to the aid of the increasingly desperate German Jews.

Nazi Germany initially adopted a policy of deporting Jews to other countries, to rid itself of them and achieve its aim of racial purity. But as Germany gained control over much of Europe during World War II, deportation was no longer practical. Their "final solution" to the Jewish problem was to exterminate the entire Jewish population of

Europe. Millions of men, women, and children were rounded up and transported to concentration camps in various parts of central and eastern Europe, where they were murdered on an industrial scale. Six million Jews lost their lives in the genocide. An equal number of other "undesirables," including gypsies, mentally handicapped people, homosexuals, and political activists were exterminated in the same way. This dark episode in twentieth-century history is known as the Holocaust.

Nazi Germany's treatment of the Jews hastened the campaign for the establishment of a Jewish homeland in Israel, a place where the world's Jews hoped to find a safe home, free from fear or oppression.

The Origins of Israel

After World War II ended, the newly formed United Nations tried to solve the problem by dividing Palestine into Jewish and Arab territories in 1947. The British gave up control over Palestine May 14, 1948, and Jews in Palestine immediately announced the creation of the State of Israel. This led to a two-year war with the neighboring Arab countries before Israel won its freedom.

After Israel was established, many Jews in other countries began moving to Israel. Today Israel is one of the few democracies in the Middle East, although it is often criticized by other countries for its treatment of Palestinian Arabs living within its borders. Israel's flag is white with a blue strip top and bottom, and a blue Star of David (a six–pointed star symbol) in the middle.

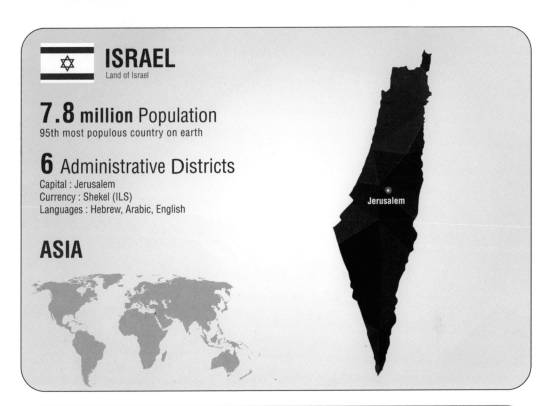

ISRAEL
Land of Israel

7.8 million Population
95th most populous country on earth

6 Administrative Districts
Capital : Jerusalem
Currency : Shekel (ILS)
Languages : Hebrew, Arabic, English

ASIA

Jerusalem

Text-Dependent Questions

1. Under what ruler did the ancient Kingdom of Israel achieve its greatest glory?
2. What is the tetragrammaton?
3. When was the modern State of Israel founded?

Research Project

Using the Internet or your school library, research the life of an important figure from the early days of Judaism, such as Abraham, Isaac, Jacob, Joseph, Moses, King David, Solomon, or one of the prophets. Write a two-page report about this person and present it to your class.

 ## Words to Understand in This Chapter

ark—in a synagogue, the cupboard or curtained alcove where the Torah scrolls are kept. In biblical times, the stone tablets of the Law were carried in a special Ark or chest with carrying poles.

Ashkenazic Jews—Jews originating from Germany, France, and eastern Europe.

bimah—a raised platform in a synagogue where the Torah is read.

cheder—a part-time religious school for children, usually held at a synagogue.

minyan—the quorum, or minimum number of people, who must be present for public worship in a synagogue.

Orthodox—traditional practice of Judaism which requires strict observance of commandments and customs.

Sephardic Jews—a term describing Jewish people who originated from the Iberian Peninsula (Spain and Portugal).

tallit—a prayer shawl.

tzitzit—fringes on the corners of the *tallit*, or prayer shawl.

yeshiva—a Jewish school that offers both secular and religious classes.

Judaism is more than just a religion. It is the entire culture, history, and civilization of the Jewish people.

3 Judaism in the Modern Day

The core beliefs and customs of Judaism are shared by all Jews, but some Jews believe that the laws and customs can be modified or re-interpreted to reflect changes in society. As a result, today there are three separate groups within Judaism, and each has come to a different conclusion about what being Jewish means. The main movements within Judaism are known as Orthodox, Reform, or Liberal (UK and Europe) or Orthodox, Conservative, and Reform (U.S.A.).

Orthodox Jews are the most traditional. They conduct services in Hebrew and observe the laws of the Torah to the letter. Within Orthodox Judaism, Hassidic Jews are the most traditional. The men wear black coats and hats modeled on clothing from eighteenth-century Poland where the

Orthodox Jews generally wear dark clothes and brimmed hats. They do not cut the hair on the sides of their heads, instead allowing it to grow into curly strands called peyot. This is because of a mitzvah in the Torah that tells Jews not to cut this hair.

movement began. Lubavitch Hassidism, often known simply as Lubavitch, is an international organization that encourages non-Orthodox Jews to return to observing traditional practices.

The Conservative movement (known as "Reform Judaism" in the United Kingdom and Europe) is quite traditional in most respects, but Conservative Jews are more relaxed about some of the laws. They do not follow all the dietary laws or those relating to not working on Shabbat.

Reform Judaism (known as "Liberal Judaism" in the United Kingdom at Europe) is even more relaxed about religious practices. In a Reform synagogue, the local language can be used for services along with Hebrew. Conservative and Reform communities also allow a more prominent role for women, who can become rabbis.

The largest organized grouping of Jews in the world is the World Union for Progressive Judaism, to which the large majority of the world's Conservative and Reform synagogues belong. Along with the American Conservative Movement, they comprise more than a third of the world's

Ashkenazic and Sephardic Jews

Historically, Jews tend to be divided into two main world groupings, based on their ethnicity and culture: *Ashkenazic* and *Sephardic*. These two groups of Jews have different languages, customs, and diets, because they were influenced by different cultures.

Ashkenazi is a name given to people descended from diaspora Jews who lived in central and eastern Europe during the time of the Roman Empire. (The name *Ashkenazi* comes from the Hebrew word for Germany.) Today, about 80 percent of Jews are Ashkenazic, including most American Jews.

The Sephardim are the Jews whose ancestors lived on the Iberian Peninsula (modern-day Spain and Portugal; the word Sephardim comes from the Hebrew word for this region.) when it was part of the Roman Empire. After the fall of the empire, Jewish communities continued to live on the Iberian Peninsula under the rule of the Muslim Moors, who invaded from North Africa. In the late fifteenth century, after the Moorish states were conquered by European Christians, both Jews and Muslims were driven out of the Iberian Peninsula. The Sephardic Jews were dispersed into North Africa and parts of southern Europe.

There are small groups of Jews who are neither Ashkenazic nor Sephardic. Cut off from mainstream Jewish culture, they developed independently. They include the Falasha of Ethiopia, the Mizrahim of Asia, and the Yemenite Jews. Due to persecution, most of these Jews have left their traditional homelands and now live in Israel.

14 million Jews. The rest are divided between secular, non-observant Jews, and a number of Orthodox and ultra-Orthodox groups.

Worship in the Synagogue

Whether a Jew follows the Orthodox, Conservative, or Reform movements, the synagogue is the center of their religious community, just as the home is the focus of the family. Both have important roles as places of prayer and reflection.

In Orthodox synagogues, services are held in Hebrew and men primarily lead the services. Orthodox services will have a choir and a cantor, but no musical accompaniment. In Conservative and Reform synagogues, about half of the service is in Hebrew while half can be in the local language (for example, often this is English in the United States). In Conservative and Reform services, Jewish women are permitted to participate to a greater degree, and there is also more community prayer and worship. An organ may also be played during Conservative or Reform services.

Prayers are said in the synagogue every day during the week, with special prayers on Shabbats and festival days. Daily prayers are said three times—in the morning (*Shacharit*), afternoon (*Minchah*), and evening (*Ma'ariv*). Traditionally, men go to their synagogue to pray as often as possible, because they are expected to pray in the company of others. Public worship in a synagogue can only happen when at least ten adults are present. In Orthodox synagogues, this *minyan* ("quorum" or "number") must be all men. In non-Orthodox synagogues, women can be included in the *minyan*.

When people gather at the synagogue for a service, they sit around, or in front of, a raised platform, or *bimah*, where the Torah and prayers are read. There is a different Torah reading for each week of the year. The Torah is usually read on Mondays, Thursdays, Shabbats, and some holidays.

The synagogue's Torah is handwritten on parchment scrolls that are normally kept in a cupboard called the Aron

In an Orthodox synagogue, the **ner tamid** *("eternal light") commemorates a light in the original Temple in Jerusalem that was always lit, symbolizing God's presence. The* **bimah** *(center) is a raised platform where the Torah and prayers are read. The* **Aron** hakodesh *("holy ark," left) is a cupboard where the Torah scrolls are kept.*

During most synagogue services, the Torah scrolls are taken from the ark and paraded round the main hall before being taken to the **bimah** *to be read. The Torah scrolls are handwritten parchment scrolls containing the text of the Torah.*

hakodesh ("Holy Ark"). The *ark* is usually fixed to the wall of the synagogue that faces Jerusalem. When the Torah is read, it must not be touched, partly out of respect and partly to protect the precious parchment from oils and acids on the readers' skin. The person saying the reading uses a pointer to follow the words. To be invited to read from the Torah is a great honor, called an *aliyah*.

Most synagogues have a rabbi ("teacher"), but it is not vital for a synagogue to have one. A rabbi does not have any more authority to perform rituals than any other male member of the congregation. The rabbi attends to the religious needs of the community. Orthodox rabbis are always men, while Reform and Liberal rabbis may be women. Traditionally, a rabbi is educated in Jewish Law and is therefore able to settle disputes that require interpretation of religious law.

In Orthodox synagogues, men and women in the congregation are separated by a screen. In Conservative and Reform synagogues, they are free to sit together. Young children can sit with either parent. Morning service usually begins with a series of blessings, followed by psalms, hymns, and prayers. Prayers are often sung and some synagogues have a cantor who is trained in traditional prayer singing.

The daily prayers are printed together in a book called the *siddur*. After *Shema*, the oldest daily prayer, the most important is *Kaddish*, often called the prayer for the dead, or the mourner's prayer, because it is also said during mourning. In all synagogues, *Kaddish* is recited in its original language, Aramaic.

Worship at Home

Judaism is a way of life, so worship and prayer are not just for special occasions or rituals. Every day is an opportunity for prayer. Worship in the synagogue is an obligation, but prayers are also said at home. Traditionally, Jews pray three times a day at home, just as they do at the synagogue. Prayers are also said before and after each meal. Each type of food has its own blessing. Many of the normal everyday events, such as getting up and going to bed, have their own blessings too.

The front door and main rooms in a Jewish home traditionally have a small box fixed to the right-hand doorpost. Placing them there is a commandment. They are called *mezuzot* (which means "doorposts") and they contain two passages from the Torah, handwritten on small pieces of parchment. Their presence is a constant reminder of God's presence in the home, and the family's obligations to God. When someone enters a room, he or she touches the *mezuzah* (the singular of *mezuzot*) and then kisses the fingers that touched it. Some *mezuzah* cases are quite plain, but others are very elaborately decorated. When a family moves house, the mezuzot are normally removed and taken to the new house. When they are fixed in place again, there is a dedication ceremony to mark the event.

Keeping Shabbat

Jews are commanded by God to observe Shabbat as a special day of rest, worship, reflection, and spiritual enrichment. It echoes the account of creation in the Book of Genesis, when God rested from His labors in creating the heavens and the Earth and everything in them. The Jewish Shabbat is Saturday, the seventh day of the week.

Jews are not permitted to work on Shabbat. Not working means more than not going to work. It means not doing anything that involves creating something, just as God refrained from creating anything on the seventh day. Forbidden activities include weaving, sewing, building, making a fire, playing sport, driving a car, cooking, or even carrying something outdoors. Orthodox Jews observe these prohibitions very strictly.

Shabbat begins at sunset on Friday evening. The woman of the house lights two candles and says a Shabbat blessing. When the men return from the synagogue, pieces of a fresh loaf of eggy bread, called *challah*, are cut, salted, and eaten, and a glass of wine is shared, with blessings, to honor the beginning of Shabbat. The man of the house says

The two candles on the Shabbat table represent the two commandments to remember and observe the sabbath. The Shabbat table should also be set with a glass of wine and at least two loaves of challah *bread.*

Educational Video

Scan here to learn about the Shabbat blessings over candles, wine and bread.

a prayer called Kiddush and the family sits down to dinner.

The following morning, the family attends the Shabbat service at the synagogue, which can last for several hours. They return home for a meal, traditionally a type of stew called *cholent*. This stew is generally prepared the day before, so no food has to be made on Shabbat. The rest of the day is taken up with Torah study, conversation, and leisure activities.

Shabbat ends at sunset. More blessings are said over candles, wine, and spices to mark the end of the day and the start of a new week.

It can be difficult for some Orthodox Jews to observe Shabbat because so many activities are forbidden. It is not permitted to push a baby-buggy or wheelchair outside the home, for example, making it difficult for mothers and disabled people to get to their synagogue. The solution is an *eruv* (meaning to "join" or "mix"). When part of a Jewish community is designated as an *eruv*, the private and public spaces within it are considered to be joined together, and all of them are treated as one large private space. Within the *eruv*, people can do things on the Shabbat that are normally forbidden outdoors. This is common in the modern State of Israel, where every town has an eruv, but relatively rare elsewhere in the world. Some major cities with significant

Jewish populations, such as New York and London, have established an *eruv*.

Religious Clothing

It is common for observant Jews to cover their heads, especially in prayer. Men traditionally wear a small skullcap, from waking to going to bed. Its Hebrew name is a *kippah*; the Yiddish name is the more familiar yarmulke. When men go outdoors, they sometimes wear a proper hat on top of the yarmulke. Orthodox women who are, or have been, married wear a *sheitel* (a wig) or a scarf. A woman who has never been married does not have to cover her head.

An Orthodox Jewish man prays at the Western Wall while wearing a yarmulke and **tallit** *(prayer shaw).* **Tefillin** *are bound to his right arm and head with leather straps.*

A family wearing traditional clothing leaves a worship service in Jerusalem.

Traditional clothes are worn and historic customs are observed during worship. Men wear a *tallit*, or prayer shawl. The prayer shawl itself has no meaning, but the fringes or tassels at its corners do. The Torah tells Jews to wear *tzitzit* ("fringes") at the corners of garments as a reminder of the Ten Commandments. Originally, twisted threads were added to normal clothes. Later, when Jews moved to other countries with different clothing styles, they adopted the prayer shawl specifically to carry the corner fringes. Orthodox Jewish men also wear a fringed undergarment at all times.

When they pray, Orthodox Jewish men bind a small leather pouch to their forehead and another to their arm with leather straps. These *tefillin* contain handwritten Torah texts on parchment. Binding them to head and arm is intended to keep God's Word close to the mind and the heart during prayer.

Religious Education

For children in Jewish families, religious education begins in the home. Both parents participate in teaching their children about the Jewish faith and culture, although mothers are traditionally considered to be the Jewish family's educators. Simply living according to Jewish traditions, which

The Torah commands that **tefillin** *should be worn when praying, to remind Jews that God brought their ancestors out of Egypt.*

A Jewish boy reads a prayer book in the school synagogue.

children witness and participate in, goes a long way to instilling in children the customs of Judaism, even without any formal class-based studies.

Synagogues play an important role in education, too. They are not only places of worship, but also places where members of the Jewish community can go to learn more about their religion. Children usually attend a religious school, or *cheder* (Hebrew for "room"), at their synagogue. The classes are held after children finish their normal school day during the week or on a Sunday morning. At *cheder*, children learn the Hebrew language and study parts of the Torah and Talmud. They also learn about Jewish festivals, customs, and history. Children attend *cheder* from about five years old. Some synagogues have a kindergarten for even younger children.

Religious education need not stop on reaching adulthood. Adults who want to continue their religious studies can usually attend Torah study meetings and evening classes at the synagogue. Most synagogues also have a well-stocked library of religious books and Jewish texts that members of the community can study.

Another type of school, the *yeshiva* ("academy"), offers lessons in both academic subjects and religion. *Yeshivot* (the plural of *yeshiva*) are mainly attended by the children of ultra-Orthodox Jews who generally prefer single-faith schools if they are available. Students who want to pursue their religious studies further can attend a university or seminary to take a degree, or to train as a rabbi.

 Text-Dependent Questions

1. What are the three movements within Judaism?
2. What are Jews whose ancestors lived in central or eastern Europe called?

 Research Project

Using your school library or the internet, find out more about the tefillin. What sort of verses are included inside? How are these worn? Present your findings to the class in a two-page report.

 ## Words to Understand in This Chapter

bar mitzvah—a ceremony marking a Jewish boy's thirteenth birthday, when he becomes responsible for his own actions under Jewish religious law.

bat mitzvah—a girl's coming of age, at twelve years old, celebrated in many Reform and Conservative Jewish communities.

chuppah—the canopy under which a Jewish couple stands during their marriage ceremony.

kashrut—the Jewish dietary laws.

kosher—food allowed to be eaten under Jewish religious law.

mikveh—a ritual bath used for spiritual cleansing.

terefah—food that is not allowed to be eaten, according to Jewish dietary laws.

A Jewish man helps his thirteen-year-old son put on a tallit before his Bar Mitzvah ritual.

4 Rites and Traditions

Jewish identity is reinforced by the many rituals and traditions that have been handed down from antiquity. These were especially important to Jews at times when they did not have a homeland to help establish their identity.

There are two ways to become a Jew. Someone can be born a Jew, or they can convert to Judaism. Traditionally, to be born a Jew, a baby must have a Jewish mother. The father may be either Jewish or non-Jewish. The reasoning behind this is probably that the identity of a baby's mother is always known with absolute certainty but the father's is not always certain. More liberal Jews accept someone as being Jewish if either parent is Jewish and the child is brought up as a Jew. Someone who is born a Jew cannot stop being Jewish. No matter how religious or non-religious they are, and even if they convert to another religion, in Jewish Law they do not stop being Jewish.

To convert to Judaism, it is not enough to share all the beliefs and practices of the religion. A non-Jew can become a Jew only by undergoing a formal process of conversion. The first step is to learn the Jewish laws and customs, and start living by them. A rabbi supervises the convert, who must also attend formal study classes.

The next step is to take an oral or written examination before a Beit Din, or rabbinical court. If successful, male

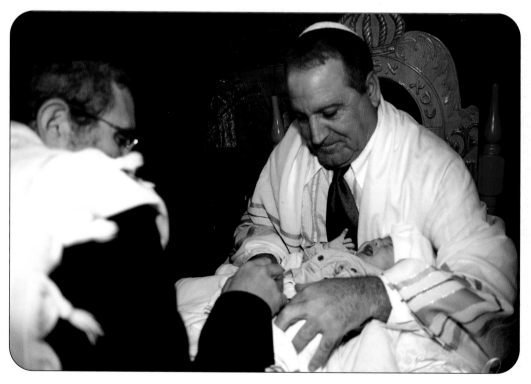

A specially trained Jew called a **mohel** *performs the circumcision ritual when a baby boy is eight days old.*

converts are then circumcised. If they are circumcised already, a symbolic drop of blood is taken. All converts are then immersed in water to symbolize their purification. They usually do this in a purpose-built water-bath, called a *mikveh*, but it could be done in a river or some other natural water. Finally, the convert is given his or her new Jewish name.

Children can be converted to Judaism too. Jewish parents might want to convert adopted children. Mixed faith (Jewish/non-Jewish) parents might want to convert children who were not born as Jews. Traditional Judaism requires a boy convert to be circumcised and both boys and girls are immersed in a *mikveh*. Other groups merely hold a naming ceremony. Children can reject the conversion if they wish at the age of twelve (girls) or thirteen (boys), when they become "adult" under Jewish Law.

Rites of Passage

Rites of passage are ceremonies performed to mark important milestones in life, such as birth, marriage, and death. On the eighth day of life, Jewish boys are ritually circumcised by having the foreskin of the penis removed. This ritual commemorates Abraham's circumcision of himself and his sons, Isaac and Ishmael, to mark their covenant with God. There is no equivalent ritual for girls, but a separate ceremony where baby boys and girls are given a Hebrew name is often held.

According to Jewish Law, boys take responsibility for their own actions from the age of thirteen. At this age, a boy

After the Bar Mitzvah ceremony, a Jewish teen is considered an adult who is morally and ethically responsible for his decisions and actions.

becomes a *Bar Mitzvah* (son of a Commandment). The equivalent age for girls is twelve. A boy's passage into religious adulthood is marked by a bar mitzvah ceremony in the synagogue. The boy reads from the Torah and often gives an explanation in front of a congregation that includes his family and friends. The ceremony is often followed by a celebration that embraces the whole family.

In Orthodox Judaism, there is no equivalent to the boy's bar mitzvah for girls. There is a ceremony called *bat chayil* ("daughter of strength"), when girls read and receive a blessing in the synagogue. In the Conservative and Reform movements, girls may have a *bat mitzvah* ceremony that is equivalent in every way to a boy's bar mitzvah. Reform Judaism also has a further ceremony at 15 or 16, called a Kabbalat Torah ("acceptance of the Torah"), when participants may conduct the entire service, and give an address affirming their faith.

Marriage and Family Life

Marriage and family life are very important to Jews. A marriage ceremony can be held in a synagogue, but it need not be. Jewish marriage is a civil contract between a man and a woman. Even so, a rabbi is normally present and two independent witnesses are required.

During the marriage ceremony, the bride and groom stand under a *chuppah*, or canopy, to symbolize their union. The bridegroom places a ring on his bride's finger. Then the *ketubbah*, or marriage contract, is read out. This lists the couple's obligations to each other. Blessings are said, then the couple drink wine, and the groom breaks a glass under his foot, probably to symbolize the destruction of the ancient Temple in Jerusalem. Family and friends will then join together to celebrate the marriage.

A marriage between a Jew and a non-Jew is not recognized as a valid marriage under traditional Jewish religious law. In Orthodox Judaism, anyone who "marries out"— marries a non-Jew—may be punished by being cut off from other Jewish people. Orthodox Jews believe that such a person cannot enter the World to Come, and their children are not recognized as Jews. Conservative and Reform Jews are more open to mixed-faith marriages.

When a Jewish marriage breaks down, the couple divorces twice—once to satisfy civil authorities and a second time according to Jewish Law. To divorce in Jewish Law, the husband obtains a document called a *get* from a Rabbinic court and gives it to his wife in the presence of witnesses. His wife must receive it willingly.

Jewish couples stand under a **chuppah,** *or canopy, during their wedding ceremony. It symbolizes the home that the couple will build together.*

At the end of the wedding ceremony, the groom stamps on a glass.

Mourning for the Dead

If a parent dies, sons and daughters traditionally tear their clothes over their heart. If another relative dies, the tear is made on the right side. In the day or two between death and burial, no one visits the mourners so they can concentrate on the dead. For seven days after the burial, the mourners do not work or do anything for pleasure. Services are held every evening. For 30 days after the death, the mourners do not go to parties or listen to music.

Parents continue mourning a dead child for 12 months by reciting the memorial prayer known as Kaddish. On

Origins of Dietary Laws

The kosher laws date back to the origins of the Jewish people 4,000 years ago. Some modern scholars have noted that the laws might have originated from practical precautions that ancient people took to avoid food poisoning. In the hot climate of the Middle East, scavenging animals such as pigs were more likely to carry diseases. Even today, pork can cause health problems in humans if it is not cooked thoroughly. The Muslim faith, which also originated in the Middle East, has similar dietary laws, called *halal*.

every anniversary of the death, a candle is lit in the home to remember the person, and their name may be mentioned in synagogue on, or near to, the actual anniversary.

Keeping Kosher

The Torah instructs Jews to follow certain dietary laws, called *kashrut*, meaning "proper" or "correct." Food that Jews are permitted to eat is called *kosher*. Foods that are considered ritually unclean, called *terefah*, are forbidden.

Generally, fruit and vegetables are *kosher*, but the meat from certain animals is not. To be *kosher*, an animal must chew the cud and have hooves that are completely divided in two. So, cows, goats, and sheep can be *kosher*, but pigs are not. Birds neither chew the cud nor have hooves, but not all of them are forbidden. *Kosher* birds include chicken, turkey,

A shochet is a butcher who has been trained to properly prepare meat so that it is kosher. Shochets are required to be devout Jews.

goose, and duck. Only fish with both fins and scales may be eaten, so all shellfish are forbidden. To make shopping easier today, packaged foods in Jewish shops often carry a label or stamp that certifies them as *kosher*.

For meat to be considered *kosher*, the animal must be killed and butchered following a process known as *shehitah*. The animal's throat is cut and blood is drained from its body. The meat is then soaked or boiled in water, or treated with salt, to draw out even more of the blood. The ancient Jews believed that blood contained the life essence of an animal, so it is prohibited.

Katz's Delicatessen, established in 1888, is a famous restaurant known for its pastrami sandwiches on the Lower East Side of Manhattan. Jewish immigrants to the United States who came from eastern Europe popularized delicatessens, which are stores that sell foreign or unusual foods. Often, the foods at a deli are prepared according to kosher guidelines.

Strict rules govern the preparation of *kosher* food. In a *kosher* kitchen, meat and dairy products must be kept apart. They are prepared and cooked separately, using separate sets of crockery and utensils. These pots, pans, and utensils are washed in two different sinks, dried with different towels and stored in different cupboards.

Although some foods and dishes are common to all Jews, there is no single Jewish cuisine or style of cooking. Jews who settled in different parts of the world adapted their diet and recipes to make use of local produce and cooking styles.

 ## Text-Dependent Questions

1. At what age does a Jewish boy become a Bar Mitzvah?
2. What is the ketubbah? What does it list?
3. If a food is designated *terefah*, what does that mean?

 ## Research Project

Using your school library or the internet, research the question, "Should you give to charity?" One perspective is that the world is unfair—the three wealthiest people in the world have more money than the 48 poorest countries combined, and millions of children die each year from poverty-related illnesses. So those who have more than they need should help those who lack enough resources to meet even basic needs. On the other hand, people deserve the money they have earned and should be able to spend it as they wish. Some people feel that charity demeans people and makes them dependent on others. Present your conclusion in a two-page report, providing examples from your research that support your answer.

Words to Understand in This Chapter

Rosh Hashanah—the Jewish New year. It is followed by the "Ten Days of Penitence," leading up to Yom Kippur.

sukkah—a temporary shelter made for the festival of Sukkot.

Yom Kippur—the Jewish Day of Atonement.

A family sits round the Seder table, about to celebrate the Passover traditions and meal.

5 Major and Minor Festivals

The Jewish year is punctuated with festivals that commemorate important events in Jewish history. Orthodox Jews observe a few more of these festivals than do non-Orthodox Jews. Many of these festivals are associated with special events and experiences, and have special foods.

The five major Jewish festivals include *Rosh Hashanah* (the Jewish New Year), *Yom Kippur* (the Day of Atonement), Sukkot (the Feast of Tabernacles), Pesach (Passover), and Shavuot (the Festival of Weeks). Their observance is required by the Torah.

Calculating Festival Dates

Jewish festivals can be celebrated on different dates from year to year. This is because the dates of these festivals are set according to the traditional Jewish calendar, which is quite different from the twelve-month calendar that most Americans are familiar with.

The United States, like most of the world, uses the Gregorian solar calendar, which is based on the sun's 365-day journey around the Earth. However, the Jewish calendar is based on the cycles of the moon, with each of the twelve months beginning at a new moon. This is called a lunar year, and is 10 or 11 days shorter than the solar year. Because of this, the lunar calendar dates gradually drift more and more out of agreement with the solar calendar. If no adjustment were made, Jewish festivals would occur about 11 days earlier every year. Festivals tied to a season would soon end up in the wrong season. Harvest festivals, typically celebrated in autumn, could instead occur in midsummer or even spring, for example.

To bring the solar and lunar calendars into agreement, the years of the Jewish calendar are divided into 19-year cycles and an extra month (Adar II) is added in the third, sixth, eighth, eleventh, fourteenth, seventeenth, and nineteenth years. Further small adjustments are made from year to year to make sure that festivals are kept separate from Shabbats, so that observing them or preparing for them does not interfere with keeping Shabbat. All of these adjustments, which vary from year to year, mean that each year Jewish festivals usually fall on different dates in the standard calendar. The solar dates of the various festivals and commemorative days are calculated and printed many years ahead of time.

Months of the Jewish Calendar

The names of the months in the Jewish calendar were originally Hebrew, but during the exile in Babylon, Babylonian names were adopted and they are still used today.

1. Nissan (30 days)
2. Iyar (29 days)
3. Sivan (30 days)
4. Tammuz (29 days)
5. Av (30 days)
6. Elul (29 days)
7. Tishri (30 days)
8. Cheshvan (29 or 30 days)
9. Kislev (30 or 29 days)
10. Tevet (29 days)
11. Shevat (30 days)
12. Adar (29 days)

Because of the difference between the lunar and solar years, the Jewish calendar provides for seven "leap months" every nineteen years. The leap month is inserted into the Jewish calendar between Shevat and Adar, and lasts for 30 days. It is known as Adar Aleph, while the final month of the year is then called Adar Bet.

The Jewish calendar begins with the month of Nissan, which occurs in March or April, but the year number does not change until the Jewish New Year is celebrated during the seventh month of Tishri, which occurs in September or October according to the western calendar. In Babylon, this was the traditional start of the agricultural year.

The Jewish calendar also has a very different numbering system for the year. The year 2018 of the western calendar, for example, is equal to the year 5778 on the Jewish calendar. When the Jewish New Year, Rosh Hashanah, is celebrated on September 10, 2018, the Jewish year will become 5779.

The year on the Jewish calendar represents the number of years that have passed since creation. This was calculated many years ago by rabbis, who added up the ages given for people listed in the Tanakh. This gives a creation date of 3761 BCE, which must be added to common era (CE) dates to convert them to the Jewish year.

Major Jewish Festivals

Rosh Hashanah (1 Tishri) marks the beginning of the year, when Jews examine their lives and accept or renew their responsibilities. It begins a period of ten days of penitence leading up to Yom Kippur, the Day of Atonement.

Yom Kippur (10 Tishri) is the most sacred day of the year to Jews. It is a day for fasting, confessing one's own sins, expressing regret for past mistakes, and pardoning others. Eating, drinking, washing, using cosmetics, wearing leather shoes, and sexual activity are all forbidden on Yom Kippur. Traditionally, Jews spend most of the day in prayer in the synagogue. There, the ark is covered with a white cloth and worshippers wear white as a symbol of purity. A *shofar* (a trumpet made from a ram's horn) is blown to mark the end of the day.

Sukkot means "huts." It refers to the temporary buildings that the Israelites lived in during the forty years when they wandered in the desert after the Lord brought them

During Rosh Hoshanah services, a trumpet made from a ram's horn, called the shofar, *is sounded. This reminds Jews of the ram that Abraham sacrificed in place of his son Isaac.*

out of Egypt. Jews are commanded to live in a temporary shelter called a *sukkah* for seven days. A *sukkah* must have three walls and a roof. The roof should be made from something that once grew from the ground, such as reeds or tree branches, and should be laid loosely so that the stars are visible through gaps. During Sukkot, four kinds of plants (a palm branch, three myrtle twigs, two willow branches, and a citron fruit, called etrog) are waved in every direction during synagogue services to acknowledge that God is everywhere. Very orthodox Jews will try to sleep in the *sukkah*.

A Jewish family builds a shelter on the eve of the Jewish holiday Sukkot in Netivot, Israel.

The festival of Sukkot is celebrated five days after Yom Kippur (15–21 Tishri), and it is a reminder to Jewish people to be grateful for the harvest.

Pesach celebrates the deliverance of the Israelite people from slavery in Egypt. Its name, meaning Passover, commemorates the time when Israelite homes were passed over during the slaughter of the first-born in Egypt. Unleavened bread, called matzah, is eaten on the first night to echo the diet of unleavened bread eaten by the Israelites fleeing from

Egypt. This festival is observed in the springtime, with the celebration beginning on 15 Nissan and lasting for seven or eight days.

Shavuot (6–7 Sivan) was originally an agricultural festival, but it also commemorates the giving of the Torah to the Jewish people. It is called the Festival of Weeks because it comes exactly seven weeks after the second day of Passover.

In addition, there are several minor festivals, including Hannukah (25 Kislev–3 Tevet) and Purim (14 Adar). The

Preparing foods for Passover, when no yeast is allowed. Foods for Passover are prepared in kitchens or using dishes specially set aside for the festival, when any substance related to leavened bread is not permitted.

Educational Video

For a short video on the Passover Seder, click here:

minor festivals are not commanded in the Torah, but they commemorate important events from Jewish history. Hannukah, which occurs in December, commemorates the recapture of the Jerusalem Temple in 165 BCE by a Jewish army. Purim commemorates an incident in which the Jewish queen Esther saved her people from a Persian plot to destroy them.

Not all of the holidays celebrated by Jews have ancient roots. The State of Israel celebrates several modern holidays every year. Yom Ha-Shoah (27 Nissan) is a day of remembrance for those who died during the Holocaust. Yom Ha-Zikkaron (4 Iyar) is similar to the American Memorial Day, as it commemorates soldiers who died fighting for Israel. The next day (5 Iyar) is Yom Ha-Atzmaut—Israel's Independence Day, the anniversary of the day when the new State of Israel was proclaimed in 1948. Finally, Yom Yerushalayim, observed on 28 Iyar, celebrates the reunification of Jerusalem by Israel after it was recaptured from Arab forces during the June 1967 War.

Special Foods

The Torah lays down strict rules for the types of food that Jews may eat and how they must be prepared. Most festivals and celebrations are accompanied by special foods. It is

A Jewish woman lights the Hannukah candles. This eight-day festival is an opportunity for families to play festive games and eat special foods.

Two-Day Rosh Hashanah

Non-Israeli Jews traditionally added an extra day to some holidays, particularly Rosh Hashanah. This is because each month in the Jewish calendar begins at a new moon. In the time of the Jewish prophets, the new month did not officially begin until at least two people in Jerusalem had seen the first glimmer of light from the new moon. Messengers were then sent out from Jerusalem to let everyone in Israel know that the new month had started.

Jews who lived within Israel received the news quickly, but those who lived in the furthest and most isolated Jewish communities were the last to hear. Because a month could be either 29 or 30 days long, diaspora Jews who had left the region could never be sure which day was the first of a new month until they received the news from the official messengers from Jerusalem. So, to be certain that they observed all the required customs at the right times, diaspora Jews were instructed to celebrate them on both of the possible days. This is sometimes referred to as *yoma arichta*, "the long day."

traditional to eat dairy dishes during the festival of Shavuot. Apples or bread dipped in honey are traditional at Rosh Hashanah. Potato cakes called *latkes* are served during Hannukah, and filled cookies called *hamentaschen* are served during Purim. Traditional meals begin with breaking bread, usually a sweet, eggy bread called *challah*.

Although Jews all over the world observe the same holidays and customs, there can be slight differences in the way they are celebrated. For example, some foods associated with festivals may vary depending on the local crops or produce. For example, Sephardic Jews celebrate Hannukah with fried donuts called *bunuelos*, instead of the potato pancakes prepared and eaten by Ashkenazim on that holiday.

 ## Text-Dependent Questions

1. What are the five major Jewish festivals?
2. What are two examples of minor festivals?
3. How does the Jewish calendar differ from the calendar most people in the United States and other western nations use?

 ## Research Project

Using the Internet or your school library, do some research to answer the question "Do religious believers need a special place of worship?" Those who agree will say that believers should be allowed to give God their very best, whatever it costs. The design of the building can create a setting that helps people to worship. Those who disagree with this perspective believe that it is not right to spend money on places of worship when people are starving all over the world. Moreover, they contend, if God is everywhere, what need is there for special places of worship? Present your conclusion in a two-page report, providing examples from your research that support your answer.

 Words to Understand in This Chapter

euthanasia—the painless killing of a patient who is suffering from an incurable and painful disease or condition. The practice is illegal in most countries.

ultra-Orthodox—a term used to describe Orthodox Jews who reject many aspects of the modern world, including television and the Internet. Those who are ultra-Orthodox, also called Haredi, attempt to practice the Jewish faith as it was in ancient times to the greatest extent that they can.

Israeli forces chase Palestinians after a protest in the West Bank city of Hebron. Many Jews are uncomfortable with the Israeli occupation of the West Bank, viewing it as a challenge to the ethics of Judaism.

6 Challenges of the Modern World

Anti-Semitism is still widespread throughout the world, but there is not the same pressure on Jews to emigrate to Israel for protection today as there was in the 1930s and 1940s. Even so, Jews all over the world have a strong emotional attachment to Israel. They are generally united in their support for Israel, although there are disagreements and divisions, even within Israel itself.

Some Israelis are Orthodox or *ultra-Orthodox*, others are more liberal, and yet others are secular. Some are Ashkenazic, others are Sephardic. Some have lived in Israel since its foundation, while others have arrived much more recently. Some survived the Holocaust, others have never experienced such brutal persecution. There are tensions between some of these groups, who have different ideas about what Israel should be, how it should be governed, how Jews should live, and how Israel should relate to the Palestinians and the neighboring Arab countries.

Today, among most faiths and communities, more marriages end in divorce, young people are more independent, and families are less close-knit. Scientific advances have led to new medical techniques that make it possible to create life in new ways. These and other aspects of modern life challenge those trying to live within Jewish Law.

Abortion and Birth Control

Judaism places great value on life. The use of condoms or other contraceptive methods is forbidden by the commandments, but these only apply to men. So, contraception is not forbidden for Jewish women.

Abortion is allowed in certain circumstances. A Jewish woman may have an abortion if continuing with the pregnancy would endanger her life. She may also have an abortion if it is necessary for her psychological welfare. A pregnancy that resulted from rape, for example, could be terminated because forcing the woman to carry the unwanted baby would inflict unacceptable mental cruelty on her. However, abortion is not allowed for reasons of sex selection or convenience.

Judaism and Homosexuality

Orthodox Jews say the Bible prohibits homosexuality and so it must always be forbidden. That view is not shared by all branches of Judaism. In 1990, the Central Conference of

Jews are divided on the issue of same-sex marriages. These unions are opposed by Orthodox Jews, such as these protesting at New York's annual Gay Pride Parade (bottom). However, Conservative and Reform Jews are more tolerant of the practice. (Right) A rabbi performs a same-sex marriage.

American Rabbis, a Reform Jewish organization, agreed to ordain gay rabbis. In 2000, the same organization voted to recognize gay and lesbian relationships. Individual rabbis had been blessing gay unions in synagogues for some time. Reform Jews believe that gay people are created by God and so the love they show for each other is just as valid as the love expressed by a straight couple. Conservative Jewish organizations began ordaining gay rabbis in 2007, and voted to approve performing same-sex marriages in 2013.

Alcohol and Drug Use

Many of the rituals and ceremonies of Judaism are traditionally accompanied by wine, but it is not compulsory to drink wine. Grape juice is just as acceptable as wine, so Jews who do not wish to consume alcohol need not drink wine at all.

In general, Jews are forbidden from doing anything harmful to their bodies, so excessive drinking, smoking, or taking harmful drugs is forbidden. Jews are also commanded to obey the law of the land unless it breaks religious law, so using illegal drugs like marijuana or heroin, or driving while under the influence of alcohol are not allowed.

Gambling

Historically, Jews who indulged in gambling were not allowed to be witnesses in Rabbinic courts. This appears to condemn gambling. Yet, today, some synagogues, especially in the United States, derive income from activities that involve gambling, such as bingo or other games of chance.

The answer is that, in general, gambling is not frowned upon unless it becomes an addiction or leads to problems. In that case, it would break the commandments instructing Jews not to do anything harmful or dangerous to themselves or other people.

The Sanctity of Life

Jews believe that nothing must be done to end life prematurely, yet the taking of life is sometimes unavoidable in order to save a life or in time of war. There are also times when it seems kinder to bring life to a close prematurely to end suffering. How does Judaism deal with these issues?

Wine is part of many Jewish ceremonies and traditions. The Torah does caution Jews to drink alcohol in moderation.

Educational Video

Scan for a short video explaining the Purim festival.

Traditionally, Jews believe that killing is forbidden and that peace is better than war. When Jews are attacked, Jewish Law commands them to fight back and, if necessary, kill in self-defense. Murder—deliberate premeditated killing—is a different matter. Murder is always wrong.

What about *euthanasia*—deliberately ending someone's life as an act of mercy? Is this a permitted killing or is it murder? According to the Torah, there is no distinction between different qualities of life. In general, life must always be preserved. So, a life must run its natural course and therefore euthanasia is wrong. Some more liberal rabbis have judged that medical treatment or food can be withdrawn from a terminally ill person in a coma and very close to death, as long as this is not against the person's previously expressed wishes. It is allowed, because doing so does not interfere with nature. In the same way, a life support machine can be switched off, because doing so merely allows nature to take its course.

Capital Punishment

In ancient times, when Jews sat in judgement on each other, people were sometimes sentenced to death, but this was very rare. Jews believed that punishments should not be handed out through hatred or revenge, but rather to demonstrate to the community how unacceptable certain crimes were.

Today, Jews live in many different countries around the world, with different policies on capital punishment. Jews accept that governments have the right to impose capital punishment in their legal systems. Many Jews are opposed to capital punishment because it has always been the penalty of last resort for only the most exceptional cases. In addition, if a mistake is made and an innocent person is executed, it is impossible to go back and put things right. For all these reasons, many Jews are personally opposed to capital punishment.

 Text-Dependent Questions

1. What attitude do Orthodox Jews have toward homosexuality and gay marriage? How does this attitude differ from the opinions of Reform Jews?
2. How does Judaism view gambling or alcohol use?

 Research Project

Using the Internet or your school library, do some research to answer the question, "Is violence ever justified? On one hand, some people argue that the principle of "an eye for an eye" expressed in the Torah would leave the whole world blind. If people are strong enough, they contend, they can overcome evil with love. Others believe that while violence is wrong, it may also be the lesser of two evils—for example, it is good to overthrow a dictator whose actions cause innocent people to suffer. Present your conclusion in a two-page report, providing examples from your research that support your answer.

Religious Demographics

U.S. & Canada about 5.6 million people

Canada about 25 million people

U.S. about 225 million people

U.S. about 0.575 million

North and South America about 10 million people

Latin America about 543 million people

Europe about 2.1 million people

Europe about 0.5 million people

Europe about 550 million people

Europe about 50 million people

Israel about 5.6 million people

Africa about 518 million people

Africa about 475 million people

Asia about 1179 million people

Asia about 350 million people

India about 18 million people

Asia about 950 million people

Asia about 550 million people

Australia and Oceania about 24 million people

Australia and Oceania about 0.7 million people

Christians
about 2.2 billion people

Muslims
about 1.6 billion people

Sikh
about 23 million people

Hindus
about 1 billion people

Jews
about 14 million people

Buddhist
about 576 million people

Christian 31.5%	Islam 22.3%	No religion 15.4%	Hindu 14.0%	Buddhist 5.3%	Sikhism 0.3%	Judaism 0.2%	Others 11%

Hinduism

Founded
Developed gradually in prehistoric times

Number of followers
Around 1 billion

Holy Places
River Ganges, especially at Varanasi
(Benares). Several other places in India

Holy Books
Vedas, Upanishads,
Mahabharata, Rarnayana

Holy Symbol
Aum

Buddhism

Founded
535 BCE in Northern India

Number of followers
Around 576 million

Holy Places
Bodh Gaya, Sarnath, both in northern India

Holy Books
Tripitaka

Holy Symbol
Eight-spoked wheel

Sikhism

Founded
Northwest India, 15th century CE

Number of followers
Around 23 million

Holy Places
There are five important, takhts, or seats of
high authority: in Amritsar, Patna Sahib,
Anandpur Sahib, Nanded, and Talwandi

Holy Books
The Guru Granth Sahib

Holy Symbol
The Khanda, the symbol
of the Khalsa

Christianity

Founded
Around 30 CE, Jerusalem

Number of followers
Around 2.2 billion

Holy Places
Jerusalem and other sites
associated with the life of Jesus

Holy Books
The Bible
(Old and New Testament)

Holy Symbol
Cross

Judaism

Founded
In what is now Israel, around 2,000 BCE

Number of followers
Around 14 million

Holy Places
Jerusalem, especially
the Western Wall

Holy Books
The Torah

Holy Symbol
Seven-branched menorah (candle stand)

Islam

Founded
610 CE on the Arabian Peninsula

Number of followers
Around 1.6 billion

Holy Places
Makkah and Madinah, in Saudi Arabia

Holy Books
The Qur'an

Holy Symbol
Crescent and star

Quick Reference: Judaism

Worldwide distribution

There are around 14 million people worldwide who define themselves as religious Jews. Figures can vary widely depending on whether one takes a religious, cultural, or ethnic definition of being Jewish.

Israel is the only country with a Jewish majority, and is home to more than 6.3 million Jews. The United States has the world's second-largest Jewish population, with more than 5.7 million. This is largely due to heavy Jewish immigration from Russia and eastern Europe between 1880 and 1924. Many of these immigrants settled in New York City, and today New York has a particularly large and thriving Jewish community.

The Jewish population of European countries has fluctuated over the centuries as successive rulers tolerated or persecuted Jews. Large-scale Jewish emigration from Europe began in the nineteenth century in response to persecution and poverty especially in eastern Europe. Today, the Jewish community in France is about half a million people. Russia (185,000) and Germany (100,000) also have small but not insignificant Jewish communities.

Language

In ancient times, Jews spoke Hebrew or Aramaic. During the diaspora, Ashkenazic Jews that settled in central Europe developed a language called Yiddish, which was a mixture of Hebrew and German. When Ashkenazic Jews left their European homelands due to persecution in the nineteenth and twentieth centuries, they took Yiddish with them and it is still spoken in many Jewish communities. Sephardic Jews who lived on the Iberian Peninsula developed their own language, Ladino, which blended Spanish and Hebrew. After the foundation of the state of Israel in 1948, the Hebrew language grew in importance. Today, Hebrew is the national language of Israel.

Festivals

The Jewish calendar is lunar, but extra months are added according to a regular schedule so that festivals always fall in the proper season each year. The years are dated from the traditional Jewish dating of the creation of the world (5779 begins in September 2018).

Major Jewish festivals include the Jewish New Year, Rosh Hashanah, on 1 Tishri (September); Yom Kippur, the "Day of Atonement," on 10 Tishri (September); Sukkot, in memory of the Israelites wandering in the desert, 15–21 Tishri (Sept./Oct.); Pesach, or Passover, from 15 to 22 Nissan (March/April), which commemorates the Exodus from Egypt; and Shavuot on 6–7 Sivan (May/June), to celebrate Moses receiving the Torah. Minor festivals include Hannukah (25 Kislev–3 Tevet) and Purim (14 Adar).

Orthodox Jewish men drink and dance while celebrating Purim in the Mea Shearim neighborhood of Jerusalem. Purim remembers an incident when the Jewish queen Esther saved her people from a Persian plot to destroy them.

Judaism Timeline

ca. 2000 BCE According to Jewish and Christian religious traditions, God establishes covenant with Abraham.

ca. 1250 BCE Moses is believed to have received the Ten Commandments on Mount Sinai.

ca. 961 BCE David, the greatest king of Israel, dies.

922 BCE After the death of Solomon, Israel is divided into northern and southern kingdoms.

722 BCE The Northern Kingdom (Israel) is destroyed by the Assyrians; its people, taken in captivity, become known as the "ten lost tribes."

586 BCE Jerusalem is conquered by the Babylonian Empire. The Temple is destroyed, and many Jews are taken into exile.

539 BCE The Persians conquer Babylon, and Cyrus the Great allows Jews to return and rebuild their Temple.

516 BCE Reconstruction of the Temple is completed.

458 BCE Ezra teaches the Jews how to understand God's law.

332 BCE Alexander the Great conquers Jewish territories.

198 BCE	The Seleucids take control of Judea.
168 BCE	Jews revolt against Antiochus IV Epiphanes, eventually gaining their freedom after four years of fighting.
63 BCE	Judea becomes a Roman province.
70 CE	The Temple in Jerusalem is destroyed in retaliation for a Jewish revolt against Roman authority that began in 66 CE.
135	Roman forces put down a Jewish revolt led by Simon bar Kokhba, and retaliate by expelling many Jews from Jerusalem.
ca. 200	The Mishnah is created by Judah the Prince.
1099	European Christian knights of the First Crusade capture Jerusalem, massacre Jewish and Muslim inhabitants.
1492	Christian armies complete the "Spanish Reconquista" and expel Jews and Muslims from the Iberian Peninsula.
1516	The Jewish "ghetto" is established in Vienna.
1730	The first synagogue in America is established in New York.
1880s	Pogroms, or state-sanctioned attacks on Jews in Russia and eastern Europe lead to an increase in Jewish emigration to the United States and Canada. Over the next few decades, large numbers of Jewish immigrants are admitted to the US until the immigration laws are changed in the early 1920s.

1919	Following World War I, the defeated Ottoman Empire loses its remaining territories in the Middle East.
1920s	The arrival of thousands of Jewish settlers in Palestine causes friction with Arabs. Jewish-Arab violence continues throughout the 1930s.
1939–45	As World War II is fought, Nazi Germany attempts to exterminate all European Jews, ultimately killing an estimated 6 million.
1947	The United Nations adopts a plan to partition Palestine into two states, one Jewish and the other Palestinian Arab.
1948	The state of Israel is proclaimed in May, and Arab nations immediately attack; by the time all fighting ceases early the following year, Israel has gained control of the territory.
1967	Israel wins a decisive victory over Egypt, Syria, and Jordan in the Six-Day War.
1987	The first Palestinian *intifada*, or uprising against Israeli rule, breaks out in the occupied West Bank and Gaza Strip.
1993	The Oslo Accords between Israel and the Palestinians establish a framework for peace, including the possibility of an independent Palestinian Arab state.

2000	The second Palestinian *intifada* breaks out, derailing the peace process and inaugurating an extended cycle of violence.
2005	In August, the government of Israel unilaterally withdraws its military forces and settlers from the Gaza Strip.
2006	After Hezbollah militants from Lebanon capture two Israeli soldiers, Israel invades Lebanon and attacks Hezbollah strongholds. A ceasefire ends the war after a month.
2008	In December, the Vatican hosts a conference involving the Pontifical Council for Interfaith Dialogue and the World Islamic Call Society.
2014	Israel's military attacks Palestinians with the militant group Hamas in the Gaza Strip in retaliation for rocket and mortar attacks on targets in Israel. The conflict lasts for seven weeks.
2017	US President Donald Trump says that Israeli settlements in the West Bank are not helpful to the peace process.

Series Glossary of Key Terms

afterlife—a term that refers to a continuation of existence beyond the natural world, or after death.

BCE and CE—alternatives to the traditional Western designation of calendar eras, which used the birth of Jesus as a dividing line. BCE stands for "Before the Common Era," and is equivalent to BC ("Before Christ"). Dates labeled CE, or "Common Era," are equivalent to *Anno Domini* (AD, or "the Year of Our Lord").

chant—the rhythmic speaking or singing of words or sounds, intended to convey emotion in worship or to express the chanter's spiritual side. Chants can be conducted either on a single pitch or with a simple melody involving a limited set of notes, and often include a great deal of repetition.

creation—the beginnings of humanity, earth, life, and the universe. According to most religions, creation was a deliberate act by a supreme being.

deity (or god)—a supernatural being, usually considered to have significant power. Deities/gods are worshiped and considered sacred by human beings. Some deities are believed to control time and fate, to be the ultimate judges of human worth and behavior, and to be the designers and creators of the Earth or the universe. Others are believed to control natural phenomena, such as lightning, floods, and storms. They can assume a variety of forms, but are frequently depicted as having human or animal form, as well as specific personalities and characteristics.

hymn—a song specifically written as a song of praise, adoration or prayer, typically addressed to a god or deity.

miracle—according to many religions, a miracle is an unusual example of divine intervention in the universe by a god or deity, often one in which natural laws are overruled, suspended, or modified.

prayer—an effort to communicate with a deity or god, or another form of spiritual entity. Prayers are usually intended to offer praise, to make a request, or simply to express the person's thoughts and emotions.

prophecy—the prediction of future events, thanks to either direct or indirect communication with a deity or god. The term prophecy is also used to describe the revelation of divine will.

religion—a system of belief concerning the supernatural, sacred, or divine; and the moral codes, practices, values, institutions and rituals associated with such belief. There are many different religions in the world today.

ritual—a formal, predetermined set of symbolic actions generally performed in a particular environment at a regular, recurring interval. The actions that make up a ritual often include, but are not limited to, such things as recitation, singing, group processions, repetitive dance, and manipulation of sacred objects. The general purpose of rituals is to engage a group of people in unified worship, in order to strengthen their communal bonds.

saint—a term that refers to someone who is considered to be exceptionally virtuous and holy. It can be applied to both the living and the dead and is an acceptable term in most of the world's popular religions. A saint is held up as an example of how all other members of the religious community should act.

worship—refers to specific acts of religious praise, honor, or devotion, typically directed to a supernatural being such as a deity or god. Typical acts of worship include prayer, sacrifice, rituals, meditation, holidays and festivals, pilgrimages, hymns or psalms, the construction of temples or shrines, and the creation of idols that represent the deity.

Organizations
to Contact

Anti-Defamation League
605 Third Avenue
New York, NY 10158
Phone: (212) 885-7700
Website: www.adl.org

American Sephardi Federation
15 West Sixteenth Street
New York, NY 10011
Phone: (212) 548-4486
Website: http://sephardi.house

B'nai B'rith International
1120 20th St NW, Suite 300 N
Washington, DC 20036
Phone: (202) 857-6600
Email: info@bnaibrith.org
Website: www.bnaibrith.org

Jewish Federations of North America
Wall Street Station
PO Box 157
New York, NY 10268
Phone: (212) 284-6500
Email: info@JewishFederations.org
Website: https://jewishfederations.org

National Council of Jewish Women
475 Riverside Drive, Suite 1901
New York, NY 10115
Phone: (212) 645-4048
Fax: (212) 645-7466
Email action@ncjw.org
Website: www.ncjw.org

Union of Reform Judaism
633 Third Avenue
New York, NY 10017
Phone: (212) 650-4000
Website: www.urj.org

Rabbinical Council of America
305 Seventh Avenue, 12th Floor
New York, NY 10001
Phone: (212) 807-9000
Website: www.rabbis.org

World Jewish Congress
9th Floor, 501 Madison Avenue
New York, NY 10022
Phone: (212) 755-5770
Email: info@worldjewishcongress.org
Website: www.worldjewishcongress.org

Further Reading

Bowker, John. *World Religions: The Great Faiths Explored and Explained*. London: Dorling Kindersley Ltd., 2006.

Goldenberg, Robert. *The Origins of Judaism: From Canaan to the Rise of Islam*. New York: Cambridge University Press, 2007.

Levenson, Jon. D. *Inheriting Abraham: The Legacy of the Patriarch in Judaism, Christianity, and Islam*. Princeton, N.J.: Princeton University Press, 2014.

Mansfield, Peter. *A History of the Middle East*. 4th ed. revised and updated by Nicholas Pelham. New York: Penguin Books, 2013.

McDermott, Gerald R. *World Religions: An Indispensable Introduction*. Nashville, Tenn.: Thomas Nelson, 2011.

Schafer, Peter. *The Jewish Jesus: How Judaism and Christianity Shaped Each Other*. Princeton, N.J.: Princeton University Press, 2012.

Smith, Huston. *The World's Religions*. New York: HarperCollins, 2009.

Wenisch, Fritz. *Judaism, Christianity, and Islam: Differences, Commonalities, and Community*. 2nd ed. San Diego: Cognella Academic Publishing, 2014.

Internet Resources

www.jewfaq.org/index.shtml
Judaism 101 is an online encyclopedia of Judaism, covering Jewish beliefs, people, places, things, language, scripture, holidays, practices and customs. It is written predominantly from an Orthodox point of view.

www.jewishvirtuallibrary.org
The Jewish Virtual Library offers a comprehensive look at Jewish history from ancient to modern times, and has a number of pages dedicated to archaeology and ancient history.

www.bbc.co.uk/religion/religions/judaism
This page from the British Broadcasting Company (BBC) provides information about Jewish beliefs, customs, history, and ethics.

www.pewresearch.org/topics/jews-and-judaism
This page run by the Pew Research Center provides links to polls and articles about the opinions and attitudes of Jews in Israel, the United States, and other countries.

www.jewishencyclopedia.com
The complete contents of the twelve-volume *Jewish Encyclopedia*, originally published 1901–1906, includes much information on Judaism and figures from its history.

www.cia.gov/library/publications/the-world-factbook

The CIA World Factbook is a convenient source of basic information about any country in the world. This site includes links to a page on each country with religious, geographic, demographic, economic, and governmental data.

http://www.imj.org.il/en/

Website of the Israel Museum in Jerusalem, which features art by Jewish artists as well as exhibits on Israel and Jewish history and culture.

www.biblegateway.com

Bible Gateway is a searchable database of the Old and New Testaments of the Bible. Various translations are available, and commentaries and notes are hyperlinked to specific Bible verses of interest.

www.sacred-texts.com

The Internet Sacred Text Archive has an enormous repository of electronic texts about religion, mythology, legends and folklore, and occult and esoteric topics. Texts related to Judaism include *The Legends of the Jews*, a collection of stories (*midrash*) prepared by Rabbi Louis Ginzberg in 1909.

Index

Numbers in **bold italics** refer to captions.

34–35, 37–39, 51, 63–64, 66
and dietary rules, 46, 60,
68–71, 80
See also Judaism
Hannukah, 36, 79–80, *81*, 82, 83
Hasidic Jews, 45–46
Hebrew Bible. *See* Tanakh
Hebrews. *See* Israelites
Herod the Great, *16*, 36
history
Abraham and Sarah, 21–22
and captivity of Israelites in
Egypt, 24–27
and conquest of Canaan, 28–30
and emigration, 39, *40*, 41, 95
and establishment of Israel,
42–43
exile of Israelites, 33–34
and famine, 22, 24
under Greek rule, 35–36
and the Holocaust, 41–42
and the Kingdom of Israel,
30–33
and persecution of Jews, 39,
41–43, 47, 95
and Rabbinic Judaism, 37–39
under Roman rule, 36–37
and the "Ten Lost Tribes," 32
and the Twelve Tribes of Israel,
24, 28
See also Judaism
Holocaust, 41–42, 80
homosexuality, 86

Isaac, 22, 63, *77*
Ishmael, 22, 63
Israel, 9, 14, 24, 28
as Kingdom, 30–33
modern state of, 10, 18, 42–43,
47, 54, 80, 85–86, 95
as the Promised Land, 10, 21,
28–30
Israel (Jacob), 22, *23*, 24

Israelites, 22
captivity of, in Egypt, 24–27
and conquest of Canaan, 28–30
in exile, 33–34
under Greek and Roman rule,
35–37
and the Kingdom of Israel,
30–33
See also history

Jacob (Israel), 22, *23*, 24
Jerusalem, 10, 31, 34, 36, 37
Jewish Temple in, *7, 11*, 12, 16,
18, 31–33, 34, 36, 37, *49*, 80
Joseph, 22, 24
Joshua, 15, 28, *29*
Judah, 22, 24, 28, 32–33
Judah (kingdom), 32–33
Judah Maccabee, 36
Judah the Prince, 38
Judaism
and beliefs, 9–10, 12, 21, 33
calendar of, 73–76, 82, 96
and the commandments, 8, 10,
16–19, *21*, 28, 35, 56, 86
Conservative, 20, 39, 45, 46,
48–49, 51, 65, 66
conversion to, 62–63
and the covenant, 10, 14, 22,
32, 33, 63
and demographics, 92, 94, 95
and education, *12*, 44, 57–59
festivals in, 27, 35, 36, 72,
73–83, 96
and halakhah (Jewish Law), 8,
16–19, 34–35, 37–39, 46, 51,
60, 63–64, 66, 68–71, 80
and languages, 96
and marriage and family life,
65–66
and modern challenges, 85–91
and monotheism, 9–10, 31, 33
and prayers, 48, 51–52, 54,

67–68
Rabbinic, 37–39
Reform, 20, 39, 46, 48–49, 51, 65, 66, 88
and rituals, 51, 60, *61*, 62–71
timeline of, 98–101
Twelve Tribes of Israel, 24
women's roles in, 46, 48–49, 51, 57, 61
See also history; Orthodox Judaism; Torah
Judea (Jewish province), 36
Judges, 30

Kaddish, 51, 67–68
Kingdom of Israel, 30–33
See also Israel
Kokhba, Simon bar, 37

Law, Jewish. *See* halakhah (Jewish Law)
Liberal Judaism (UK). *See* Reform Judaism
Lubavitch Hassidism, 46

marriage and family life, 65–66
Mattathias, 36
Messiah, 8, 10, 12, 14, *32*
Mishnah, 8, 15, 38, 39
Mizrahim Jews, 47
Moses, 8, 10, 12–13, 14, 15, 16, *21*
birth of, 25
death of, 28
and the Exodus, 27–28

Nazi Germany, 42–43
Northern Kingdom, 32

oral Torah, 8, 14–15
See also Torah
Orthodox Judaism, 19, 44, 45–46, 48, 53, 54, 59, 64–65, 86, *87*
and festivals, 73, 77, 97

and marriage and family life, 65
and religious clothing, 44, 55, 56, 57, *61*
and ultra-Orthodox Judaism, 84
and worship services, 48, *49*, 51
See also Judaism

Palestine, 20, 37, 41, 42
Passover (Pesach), 27, 73, 78–79
Pentateuch. *See* Torah
plagues, 26, 27
pogroms, 39
prayers, 48, 51–52, 54, 67–68
"Promised Land," 10, 21, 28–30
See also Israel
Prophets (Tanakh), 12, 14
Purim, 79–80, 82, *97*

rabbis, *15*, 16, 33–34, 50–51, 62, 65, 88
women, 46, 51
Reform Judaism, 20, 39, 46, 48–49, 51, 65, 66, 88
See also Judaism
Reform Judaism (UK). *See* Conservative Judaism
religious clothing, 44, 55–57
research projects, 19, 43, 59, 71, 83, 91
rituals, 60, *61*, 64, 65–66, 68–71
circumcision, 62, 63
conversion to Judaism, 62–63
mourning, 51, 67–68
Roman Empire, 36–37, 47
Rosh Hashanah, 72, 73, 76, *77*, 82

same-sex marriage, *87*, 88
Sarah (Sarai), 22
Saul (King), 30
scrolls, Torah, *13*, 50–51
See also Torah
Second Temple, *16*, 34, 36, 37

About the Author

Adam Lewinsky has a doctorate in medieval literature, and has taught at colleges and universities in New England for the last twenty years. This is his first book for young people.